THE Lord's Blessings

THE Lord's Blessings

Isabel Anders

THOMAS NELSON PUBLISHERS
Nashville

Published in Nashville, Tennessee, by Oliver-Nelson Books, a division of Thomas Nelson, Inc., Publishers, and distributed in Canada by Lawson Falle, Ltd., Cambridge, Ontario.

Printed in the United States.

Library of Congress Cataloging-in-Publication Data

Anders, Isabel, 1946–
The Lord's blessings / Isabel Anders.
p. cm.
ISBN 0-8407-9171-2
1. Beatitudes. 2. Alcoholics—Religious life. 3. Alcoholics—Prayer-books and devotions—English. I. Title.
BT382.A64 1992
248.8'6—dc20 92-2284
CIP

For

Dare Cox

I would also like to express appreciation to my excellent editor, Lila Empson, and to thank the Tuesday Triangle Family Al-Anon group in Akron, Ohio.

CONTENTS

The Beatitudes

Blessed are the poor in spirit,
For theirs is the kingdom of heaven.

Blessed are those who mourn,
For they shall be comforted.

Blessed are the meek,
For they shall inherit the earth.

Blessed are those who hunger and thirst for righteousness,
For they shall be filled.

Blessed are the merciful,
For they shall obtain mercy.

Blessed are the pure in heart,
For they shall see God.

Blessed are the peacemakers,
For they shall be called sons of God.

Blessed are those who are persecuted
for righteousness' sake
For theirs is the kingdom of heaven.

—Matthew 5:3–10

LOVE, joy, peace, longsuffering, kindness, goodness, faithfulness, gentleness, self-control. Against such there is no law.

—Galatians 5:22–23

GOOD without GOD becomes O.

—From a church sign

EVERYONE who got where he is had to begin where he was.

—Richard L. Evans

To you it has been given to know the mystery of the kingdom of God; but to those who are outside, all things come in parables.

—Mark 4:11

INTRODUCTION

LIFE in recovery is a down-to-earth, choice-by-choice experience. It is more than accepting certain principles, learning a realistic approach to life, or keeping the right goals in view—as important as these things are. Living in recovery means acting, as best as we can, on what we know to be true at this stage of our growth.

We have learned that in order to put into practice our good intentions, we need Someone else to help us. It is not enough to focus on "the good" in an abstract way. We need the help of our Higher Power in order to learn how to live in love, joy, peace, patience, kindness, goodness. . . . As someone has said, "GOOD without GOD becomes O."

Can we ever say that we are good? Do we ever attain a state in which things in our lives are in the right order and perspective so that we might even call ourselves "blessed"?

This goal is one that is supported by many teachings of the Bible—by wisdom ideas in the Old Testament about the good life; and especially by Jesus in His Sermon on the Mount in Matthew 5.

In that chapter, we discover some of the most frequently misunderstood statements about goodness and blessedness—yet also some of the most helpful principles we can find for our recovery. They are commonly called the beatitudes and consist of eight prescriptions for the good, moral, and ethical life; which, when lived, bring blessing to the person following them.

Each of these beatitudes, or congratulatory exclamations, describes a blessing. Each blessing conveys a truth and insight that a particular way of being good is worthy and full of happiness for the one who experiences it.

Jesus spoke the blessings to His disciples in a teaching section of the Gospel of Matthew (Matt. 5—7). Because these guidelines (Matt. 5:3–10) are written in succinct, beautiful language and deal with ethical and moral behavior in a fresh and sometimes confusing way, they have been much studied and written about. My purpose here is to help shed some light on the practical value of these blessings for living in recovery day by day.

What does it mean to be a person who is blessed, and who is a blessing to others in today's world? One startling answer is, "To believe in God." Those of us who are in recovery have learned to live always in expectation that, no matter how rough things are at the moment, it can get better. God has promised help, guidance, and blessing as we seek to follow the teachings of Scripture and other wise advice that we are privileged to receive in our lives.

Jesus' Sermon on the Mount begins with such hopeful exclamations of joy and blessedness for that very reason: God is at work in the world. We can expect great things if we have asked God to be with us in our lives and to work in us as well. Therefore, we will want to learn all we can about what will help us in recovery, what pleases God, and how we can cooperate with this process in all of our choices.

Each of the blessings is not only a piece of wise advice—an observation of the true meaning behind appearances; it also carries an expectation of the good that is yet to come. One truth that we will discover in the Gospel is that Jesus (whose full identity was only slowly revealed through his lifetime, even to those closest to him) is King.

In the Old Testament, the one God was perceived by the people of Israel as something like an oriental ruler of their day. The duty of this sovereign was to protect and guide his people in the path of a good and productive life. Although history shows us that earthly rulers are far from fulfilling these hopes, the concept of God as a good king and a strong deliverer comes through—especially in the Psalms, Isaiah, and other prophetic writings of the Old Testament.

God, the Lord, is in the business of saving people through the divine, almighty power, but also through means of the people's own faithfulness.

This truth carries over into our understanding of what salvation truly is. In Philippians 2:12–13 Paul writes, "Work out your own salvation . . . ; for it is God who works in you both to will and to do for His good pleasure." Whatever we ask of God in our lives: salvation, healing, peace, service to others—we also must work diligently toward those ends. In the blessings we learn more of how and why this is true.

In order to show several dimensions of what is meant by both living the blessings and asking God to work in us through them, I have juxtaposed some sayings from the literature of recovery with each of Jesus' statements in this section of Matthew 5. The blessings remind us that the realization of God's work on earth is not yet acknowledged and experienced by everyone, but that God is at work and active in our lives and in the lives of others.

The principles that we have for recovery and wisdom in living day to day can help us to aim closer to Jesus' list of ideal values and practices. For we know also that each day, each moment, is part of the whole of our life. And each choice we make, in a sense, either furthers or impedes the work of God in our lives and in the lives of those around us.

The blessings speak to us not only of what is true here and now (or what ought to be the case); they also point toward greater fulfillment of God's purposes in the world, when the true value of all things will be revealed. They invite us to participate here and now in

Jesus' "exclamations of joy" that God will someday redeem and restore all creation.

Let us discover some ways we can experience blessing through our individual recovery and some means of reaching out to others and sharing the good news that will naturally result from our own healing of mind and spirit.

"Thanks be to God for His indescribable gift!"
—2 Corinthians 9:15

—Isabel Anders
Winchester, Tennessee

CHAPTER 1

YOU WILL HAVE PEACE OF MIND

Blessed are the
poor in spirit,
For theirs is the
kingdom of heaven.

Peace of mind depends on uniting myself with God in power and guidance.

BLESSED are your eyes for they see, and your ears for they hear; for assuredly, I say to you that many prophets and righteous [people] desired to see what you see, and did not see it, and to hear what you hear, and did not hear it.

—Matthew 13:16–17

TO see things as they are, the eyes must be open; to see things as other than they are, they must be open even wider. To see things as better than they are, they must be open to the full.

—Antonio Machado y Ruiz

ACCEPT your positive experiences without taking credit and you have humility. Accept your negative experiences without blame and you have serenity.

—Camden Benares

"IT'S just an experiment, Mom!" my seven-year-old daughter, Sarah, would explain—as though that compensated for the water on the bathroom floor, the sticky substance she was mixing with one of my wooden spoons, and the glob on the living room floor that seemed to be spreading its stain outward in rivulets and tiny tidal waves.

Horrified at the mess, all I could see was the time and effort it would take to clean it all up and discover what damage was irreparable and what wasn't. I had trouble in that moment giving thanks for her ever-inquiring mind, her ingenuity at putting things together, and her initiative. Someday perhaps, she could do her "experiments" in a more controlled environment than the living room, perhaps even contributing to new discoveries in the field of science. If I could somehow learn to see through these annoyances to the real Sarah and her wonderful gifts. . . .

So much of appreciating our life depends on seeing what is really there. We cannot afford to allow ourselves to be distracted by all the obstacles that get in the way of love, of valuing one another, and of finding out what God wants us to learn in any situation.

One of the most important tasks in the life of recovery is learning to see things as they truly are. The deeper we go in seeking help from God, our Higher Power, the stronger our taste will grow for truth, for peace, and for serenity. And the more we desire peace, the more we will be able to stop, look and listen to what is around us. We will begin to see other people in a less threatening light; we will learn to become kinder to ourselves at every stage of growth; yet we will also become open to new insights that can help us continue to stretch and improve, day by day.

The author of *A Day at a Time,* J. B. W., writes in the companion book, *A New Day* (p. 188):

> I considered myself a compassionate and sympathic person. My heart went out to the downtrodden and those in need; I was always on the side of the underdog. Looking back, I see that I took a great deal of pride in that character trait, even though I rarely lifted a finger to help anyone but myself. The empty feelings of empathy allowed me to rationalize on occasion that I was a good-natured, caring person. Moreover, my self-deception convinced me that since I had this one virtue, I must have had many.

> When I began my new life and gradually became willing to take an honest look at myself, this rationalization was one of the first to fall away.

This experience is a common one for those of us who are truly growing in peace and recovery. What looked okay to us yesterday may not be good enough today because we've grown! And this is to be expected if we are truly seeking guidance, if we have turned to God and asked for His help on our way.

Peace of mind depends on uniting ourselves with God in power and guidance. There is more ahead for all of us—more to see, more to experience, and more to learn every day. One way to be sure that we have consciously united ourselves with God is to read regularly the Bible as well as other devotional helps to aid us in our recovery. Through openness to God's Word we prepare our hearts to see ourselves more clearly, and we also find in the Bible a reflection of what might be in the future.

Jesus calls us, especially in the blessings, to see things not only as they are but as they might be and as they ought to be—even in this life. In fact, Jesus often used the metaphors of vision and hearing to refer to spiritual understanding. In this He echoes the prophets, who also spoke in poetic, somewhat veiled expressions to emphasize their messages. Jesus quoted the words of Isaiah when He said,

> Hearing you will hear and shall
> not understand,
> And seeing you will see and not
> perceive (Matt. 13:14).

What did Jesus and the prophet mean? Apparently, this path of choosing to grow, day by day, is not as simple a task as we might think. The fact is, when we think we are good, living pretty well, according to God's laws, we have not discovered enough truth about ourselves.

Like the Pharisees of Jesus' day, when we think we have everything right, we may be falling into the worst trap of all—pride. Such self-congratulation and smugness can inhibit growth unless we continually ask God to open our eyes further, to lead us on, and to keep us growing.

The life of recovery, and the Christian life, requires more than ethical living. As important as it is to live morally and with integrity in all our choices and actions, we also want to be people who are open to insight about ourselves and about God. Thus we will recognize our growth as a gift and not something we earned or manufactured on our own. If we can learn to accept our experiences and insights without taking credit for what we have learned, and to accept our failures without blaming ourselves or others unkindly, then we are moving closer to what Jesus wants to teach us from His blessings.

The blessings teach us through wise insights—through Jesus' values concerning "the good life"—how we can learn to have our eyes open and our ears tuned to wisdom and truth in daily life. That wisdom involves not only right acts but also self-awareness. If we think we are already good, or special, or above the rules, or spiritually advanced, we've missed the point—and the opportunity. We haven't admitted fully our helplessness, our dependence on God for everything. We're in the dark. In trying to avoid the pitfall of failure we may inadvertently fall into another chasm—that of pride.

To help all of us on the way, Jesus gave us a concentrated look at how things are and how they shall be someday in God's time. If we ask Him for open eyes, open ears, and open hearts, we will be able to see and hear what He is teaching.

"Blessed are the poor in spirit," He said. These persons will inhabit, colonize, and thrive in the coming era of peace to which He alludes. They are also the ones who are the salt and the light of the world here and now (see Matt. 5:13–14). In other words, those who know that they don't have all the answers, yet act on what they do know, will begin to understand this truth.

What does it mean to be "poor in spirit"? For those listening to Jesus' teaching, actual poverty was never far away. So Jesus' implication that poverty was a desired virtue was no doubt jarring and unpleasant. The poor people of that day thought that if only their physical, material needs were met, then they could turn their energies to other things of value—perhaps even follow Jesus. But they were encumbered, tied up with subsistence living in a poor economy, as are many people today. To some of Jesus' listeners, His admonition to seek the things of the spirit may have sounded frivolous in the face of grueling labor to survive.

But Jesus called attention to the "blessedness" of something they could understand—and so can we. This promise means more than the Old Testament concept that God as King will protect the weak and provide for their care—though that too is a promise (see Matt. 6:30–34). If God cares for the birds of the air and the grass of the field, does He not care even more for His children? Yet in order to experience this care we must trust in God's provision and not worry. How are we to discover blessedness in such a state of dependence, of poverty or helplessness?

We are to be poor in the spiritual sense—we are to desire the poverty of spirit that is an openness to what God will provide, not just what we ourselves can produce and enjoy on our own. Peace of mind depends on uniting ourselves with God's power and guidance. This is the beginning of wisdom, which is an admission of our constant need for God that brings us to true poverty of spirit and to the blessedness Jesus promises.

Such poverty, or recognition of need, reflects clearly the kind of brokenness that we experience in recovery: that all-important admission that on our own we are no better, no more successful at caring, no more expert at negotiating a good life than is anyone else. We need God. We never outgrow the need for guidance.

We think we're so sophisticated, so caring, so educated, so selfless, so right about things. Yet our world is in shambles.

It may be unappealing, even humiliating, to admit that we can't cope, that we need something else; Someone else to take the reins of our life and guide us back onto the road. But this step is absolutely essential for beginning a life of true recovery.

The psalmist expressed this poverty of spirit:

> This poor man cried out,
> and the LORD heard him,
> And saved him out of all his troubles
> (Ps. 34:6).

He looked to God alone to come to him in his difficulties. He did not expect to use his own ingenuity to find his way out of the labyrinth of confusion and despair in which he found himself. He knew the most important truth of all: he couldn't do it on his own. This poverty of spirit is the key to seeing a way out, to hearing the word of truth. It is, to quote English poet

William Blake, to take hold of the "golden string" that will lead one "on to heaven's gate, built in Jerusalem's wall."

Those who are proud of spirit—the ones who have not yet discovered their need for God—are blind to the "string" that can pull us upward. They are blind to the marvelous truth about life here and now, and the blessed life that lies ahead.

Those realities or glimpses of true recovery we have prayed to see and hear may come to us at any point. We find them reflected in our own longing to find wholeness and peace. We see them in the needs of others that we may be able to alleviate through the grace of God.

And occasionally God allows us to see things better than they are, so that we are encouraged to work for these goals as best we can. When our eyes begin to open, like the blind man Bartimaeus, whom Jesus healed, we also are enabled to follow Jesus on the road (see Mark 10:52).

Often however, everything in our instinctive nature fights the idea of "letting go and letting God." It is as though the most important truth in the world—our need for our Creator—is the hardest for us to admit. Surrender to God requires something totally foreign to our desire to control our lives, to make it better for ourselves, and to set ourselves up as Number One.

When God's Word speaks to us paradoxically of the wealth of poverty or of the blessedness of being stripped of pride and false image, we try to rationalize such truth away and excuse our self-centered behavior.

St. Augustine of Hippo wrote:

> The Word of God is thine adversary. . . . It is the adversary of thy will till it becomes the author of thy salvation. . . . It is our adversary as long as we are our own adversaries. As long as thou art thine own enemy, thou hast the word of God thine enemy; be thine own friend, and thou art in agreement with it.

We become true friends to ourselves, as St. Augustine knew, when we become friends of God.

John A. Sanford, in his book *The Kingdom Within,* writes of the inner meaning of Jesus' parables—the hidden messages that teach us of ourselves and our own blindness so that we may enter into the light of wholeness and growth God has for us. He points out also that obedience to precepts—ethical living—is not the whole of the gospel or the only step toward healing. One must also become conscious:

> Consciousness is usually represented under the symbol of a light, or a lamp, or an eye, something that denotes "seeing"; that is, psychological knowing. So Jesus says: "The lamp of the body is the eye. It follows that if

> your eye is sound, your whole body will be filled with light. But if your eye is diseased, your whole body will be all darkness" (Matt. 6:22–23). . . . All true morality springs from the clarity of consciousness.

Thus, in the blessings, we are called to see, to hear, to *become aware* of what life lived in God's peace is really like. In the following chapters we will discover how we are called to experience that peace of mind more and more, day by day, in the company of others on the way.

Afterthought

To admit I have been in the wrong is but saying that I am wiser today than I was yesterday.

—Allan Picket

Today, I want to see beyond the obvious; to value all of those I encounter in my life; to make choices which will benefit everyone concerned. Now, when my daughter wants to "experiment," we choose together the materials, the tools, the place, the time . . . and since I'm a learner too, the sky's the limit of what can be discovered together.

Pray: *Lord, open my eyes and ears to embrace Your peace now. Teach me of Your own dependence on the Father during your life on earth. May I know the true poverty of spirit that marks me as Your disciple. Amen.*

CHAPTER 2

YOU WILL BE COMFORTED

Blessed are those who mourn,
For they shall be comforted.

You can't do it alone.

FOR I am persuaded that neither death nor life, nor angels nor principalities nor powers, nor things present nor things to come, nor height nor depth, nor any other created thing, shall be able to separate us from the love of God which is in Christ Jesus our Lord.

—Romans 8:38–39

AS soon as a man turneth himself in spirit, and with his whole heart and mind entereth into the mind of God which is above time, all that ever he hath lost is restored in a moment.

—*Theologia Germanica*

THE more difficulties one has to encounter, within and without, the more significant and the higher in inspiration his life will be.

—Horace Bushnell

COMPUTERS are wonderful tools in the workplace, and now that I've learned to write with a word processor, I can hardly imagine going back to a typewriter with all the messy corrections and retyping of pages. Seeing letters light up on a dark screen has become commonplace to me, and I no longer feel such insecurity that I print out every page as I write it!

But sometimes the inevitable happens—the thunder cracks outside, and the power goes out. I lose everything in an instant, and I can retrieve only the material that I've saved electronically. If I can't remember those last sentences I was furiously constructing, it's as though they never existed.

Several times an equipment failure has caused me to lose hours of work on lessons or chapters. The words disappeared into nowhere, like lights recessed into the blackness of the screen. Consequently, I have realized that even a computer's wonderful efficiency is touched with impermanence and potential loss. Yet I plow ahead, taking chances that I won't lose anything and hoping that I gain by learning how to enjoy possible benefits and how to cut my losses and go on.

With our eyes open and our ears tuned to listen, we will have to admit to ourselves that life is difficult—hardly a bed of roses, unless you consider the thorns. We will not always succeed, even with the best intentions.

Another surprising truth we find in recovery is that often we do not know what our inner motivations really are. We may think we are gaining something, when in fact we are losing something: we are alienating others by attitudes of which we are unaware.

Even when this is not the case, others will not always accept our attempts to find inner peace or our efforts to share it with them. Circumstances will sometimes separate us from those we love, causing us to face excruciating choices that leave us feeling depleted.

In this life of recovery, we can't do it alone. Never are we more aware of our need for God than when we find ourselves stumbling and failing in our attempts to manage life. Yet our failing to win at life is actually a gift to us, a signal that more is ahead—a better life with more fullness—if we keep on. Our failures become signposts, gifts on the way, as Bill W. states it (*In God's Care,* Feb. 12):

> In God's economy, nothing is wasted. Through failure, we learn a lesson in humility which is probably needed, painful though it is.

Life brings us situations that can cause genuine sadness, even mourning—for loves we have lost, for opportunities wasted, for years and talents squandered. This world is a "vale of tears" to us at some points in our journey.

What does the Bible have to say about the lesson we can learn from our grief, from mourning that seems to engage all of our energies and waylay us in our desire for serenity now?

Jesus said in the second blessing, "Blessed are those who mourn." This understanding is not a common one. How could something so unpleasant, and even repugnant, to us as mourning be important to our recovery?

It is possible that "those who mourn" as used here in Matthew means quite literally those who are bereaved—an experience most people face in some degree, at some time. It may refer to the actual loss of a dear one's life; or it may refer to the loss of career, health, hope, or any number of good gifts.

In Jesus' time, He may have spoken especially to those who mourned the bondage of the nation Israel and the evil reign of its foes. Christians today who work for justice in the civil order can surely identify with this ongoing mourning and the desire for true freedom from oppression for all peoples.

Another dimension of mourning hinted at here relates (as do all the blessings) to the future. Some people, after seeing all that God has done in their lives, mourn in their longing for the coming future age of God's reign over heaven and earth. In that day, all will see and know the truth.

The writer of Revelation describes this day: "And I heard a loud voice from heaven saying, 'Behold, the tabernacle of God is with men, and He will dwell with them, and they shall be His people. God Himself will be with them and be their God'" (Rev. 21:3).

In the following verse, the writer understands this reign of God to bring comfort, as does the second blessing: "And God will wipe away every tear from their eyes; there shall be no more death, nor sorrow, nor crying. There shall be no more pain, for the former things have passed away" (Rev. 21:4).

This vision of what God can do for all people is appealing! Often we can live and suffer through a great deal if only we have hope; if only we know that at the end of the day, or the hour, or the week, or the month, there will be relief and comfort. We seek God's presence with us in mourning (mourning which is often appropriate, given our circumstances). And we desire the presence of others we love—family who accept us as we are, friends who will walk with us, and the wider fellowship of recovery of which we have become increasingly aware.

Joseph Addison wrote, "Friendship improves happiness, and abates misery, by doubling our joy, and dividing our grief." We may discover in our steps of recovery, that increasingly we are able to make friends and keep friends because we are able to be honest in expressing ourselves. We do not always need to be "up" or to prop others up to keep them from leaning, falling, and bringing down the whole house of cards we call our life.

Rather, we have learned that true joy grows from within, through the transformation that comes as we turn to God for help. Even if we identify strongly with those who mourn for a time, we too can believe that "weeping may endure for a night, but joy comes in the morning" (Ps. 30:5).

We may see others live through circumstances worse than those we have experienced. And many of them are still praising God in the land of the living. Perhaps we have been through similar straits before and know that no matter how tough it is right now, this too will pass.

Thus we can feel our grief for a time, allowing it to take appropriate expression in our lives. But we are never totally without comfort so long as we are seeking God daily in prayer and in His Word, praying with and for others, doing our work honestly and well, and taking it a day at a time through the valley of our grief.

The second part of this blessing says that we will be comforted. Perhaps already little details in life are reaching us in our grief—details that tend to escape our notice when all the larger things are going well. So much of the good and blessed life depends on noticing what is really there.

Amy Carmichael wrote in *His Thoughts Said . . . His Father Said . . .* (p. 51), "Doth the burning sun distress thee? There shall be a shadow from the heat. Art thou beaten by the storm? There shall be a covert for thee from storm and from rain. Or is it that thou art too weary to know why thou art so weary? Then come unto Me and I will refresh you."

When we look around us at God's world, we see that there is shelter from the storm and the rain and that we do have all that we truly need for this day. We see the beauty of life around us as well. We may begin to notice the small pleasures of flowers edging the sidewalks or the whiteness of the clouds or the sweetness of voices that speak our names.

All are gifts from the Father from whom all good things come. All those who mourn will be refreshed. Jesus said, "Come to Me, all you who labor and are heavy laden, and I will give you rest. Take My yoke upon you and learn from Me, for I am gentle and lowly in heart, and you will find rest for your souls. For My yoke is easy and My burden is light" (Matt. 11:28–30).

We can't do it alone. And we don't have to. The invitation in Scripture is to turn to God and find out what life can be like under Jesus' yoke. A yoke was a wooden bar or frame that joined two work animals for labor. It doesn't sound any more appealing than our mourning itself!

Yet Jesus promises that when He is our partner in this working relationship, life will begin to have balance. We will find rest after labor and help for our stress. We will also learn through this linked relationship what it means to follow in His way. We will not be going it alone in our life or in our steps toward recovery.

One vibrant promise to those who mourn in this life is found in Isaiah. It is another expression of God's love and concern for the brokenhearted in this life:

> He has sent Me to heal the
> brokenhearted,
> To proclaim liberty to the captives,
> And the opening of the prison to those
> who are bound;
> To proclaim the acceptable year of the
> LORD . . .
> To console those who mourn in Zion,
> To give them beauty for ashes,
> The oil of joy for mourning,
> The garment of praise for the spirit
> of heaviness;
> That they may be called trees of
> righteousness,
> The planting of the LORD,
> that He may be glorified (Isa. 61:1b–3).

Opening of the prison of the soul! Beauty for ashes! The oil of joy for mourning! To be as trees of righteousness! All of these beautiful phrases work together to refresh and comfort us as we read the promises and blessings of God's Word. And personally, we know how these words may apply and how God may act through us and through others to continue to bring peace and blessing.

Let us rejoice! We are still discovering surprising dimensions of the many good things the blessings have to offer us. The mourning that we experience for a time has a silver lining; and in fact, it is always too early to give up hope. We have not yet seen the way things really are in this world, the way they could be, and the way they will be someday. God has yet to unveil the divine plan and its glory in full measure.

To turn to God, in Christ, is to yoke ourselves with the Victor. Someday those who mourn will be the most ardent rejoicers in the Kingdom.

Afterthought

No one can claim that some things are worse than others, for everything is good in its proper place.

—Sirach 39:34 TEV

Sometimes when I lose computerized sentences to the electronic graveyard, I have to try harder to replace them, and I end up with better ideas than my original ones. What losses have you experienced that have turned out to be to your greatest benefit in later years?

Like a bird that trails a broken wing, I have come home to thee.

—Ellen Gilbert

Conquered unhappiness always lies in back of tranquility.

—David Grayson

Pray: *Lord, You have promised that You are very near to those who mourn, to those who are brokenhearted. I ask for strength through these trials, for joy in what You yet will do, for peace and comfort here and now—remembering always the needs of others also. Amen.*

CHAPTER 3

YOU WILL INHERIT THE EARTH

Blessed are
the meek,
For they shall inherit
the earth.

Easy does it. Slow motion gets you there faster.

THEREFORE let him who thinks he stands take heed lest he fall.

—1 Corinthians 10:12

NOTHING sets a person so much out of the devil's reach as humility.

—Jonathan Edwards

FLAT on your back? Best way to see heaven.

—Peter deVries

MARK Twain once said that man is the only creature who blushes—or who needs to! Have you ever been in the process of showing someone else the right way to do something—to install an appliance, or spell a word, or paint a wall—and fumbled while following your own instructions? Most of us have had this experience, and we tried either to rationalize away our failure or to prove we were right all along except that those perverse, inanimate objects got in our way.

For me, it was a lost check that I was sure that I had put in a safe place. Yet it was finally found on a countertop—under other papers. But I never do that! I was appalled at my own carelessness. Yet I did laugh, too.

This freedom to fail and to be inconsistent—to be human—comes with the help of recovery principles and the loving presence of other recovering people. We all have times when we need to smile (or wince) as we inevitably fall on our faces while trying to be perfect.

Obviously, humility is an important element in our

program of recovery. Most of us need to exercise this trait every day!

We have already seen that if we think we're doing okay—if we feel we have a handle on life, that we're flying ahead full speed on our own power—we're not likely to discover the blessings of recovery at all. And we're likely to crash at any moment.

If you think you're already on top of the mountain, be careful! The only way onward is downward. But if, in contrast, you are open to learning slowly and patiently, then the trait necessary for the journey is humility.

Humility, or meekness, is not a popular virtue. It goes along with caution, patience, endurance, slowness to anger—sometimes reluctance to act. Yet in the life of which Jesus spoke, and in our life of recovery, it is clear that we are called to a life of humility before God. We discover humility through admitting that we cannot get out of the pit of addiction, codependency, depression, hyperactivity, or self-defeating behavior by ourselves.

We may have looked successful to the rest of the world. But we knew that our own efforts were leaving us short. As someone has said, the higher a person climbs, the further he is from God. This paradox is true not only of life in Christ, in which works are not the key to heaven; but also in the life of recovery. We are called not to conquer the world tomorrow but to live today in serenity and peace.

In this way of life, "easy does it" is our best guide—especially when the goal seems unattainable, the pace of life too fast, and the demands too great. The late composer Hoagy Carmichael said it in a nutshell, "Slow motion gets you there faster."

Jesus' word of blessing, "The meek [or humble] . . . shall inherit the earth," finds its source in the Psalms:

> But those who wait on the LORD,
> They shall inherit the earth.
> For yet a little while and the
>   wicked shall be no more; . . .
> But the meek shall inherit the earth,
> And shall delight themselves
>   in the abundance of peace (Ps. 37:9–11)

Here, to be meek means to be slow to anger, sensitive to others, giving and loving toward one's neighbors. These qualities lead to improved personal relationships with others and also heal the person who exercises them. Humble persons do not rush around in a frantic effort to demonstrate how capable, nice, successful, expert, and efficient they are. Humble persons take time to reflect and think in the face of the temptation to act hastily. "Easy does it" implies an ease and comfort with oneself that leads to greater self-esteem than "Look what I've accomplished!"

Moses was an example of the meekest of men: "Now the man Moses was very humble, more than all men who were on the face of the earth" (Num. 12:3). He was not reluctant or retiring, but he was aware of his own limitations and was in the process of learning to depend on God for everything. He was one who knew the Source of power and depended on that Source to bring an enslaved people out of their bondage in Egypt.

Jesus also described himself as "gentle [meek] and lowly in heart" (Matt. 11:29). Yet as we see in his dramatic expulsion of the merchants from the temple, he was far from indecisive or weak. Rather he was guileless in thought and action: welcoming to all those of like spirit who would come to Him; and decisive and authoritative when the situation genuinely required action.

We too can learn this kind of humility—which is ultimately victory. Turning to God for guidance, listening, taking time to stop and think, and then acting with confidence is a way of following in His steps. It may mean slowing down in our own human desire to fix everything right now.

In the words of one recovery axiom, "Do only what you will not later regret." This advice is excellent for anyone aiming at the godly meekness of which Jesus spoke, which is a trait of those who are able to receive the peace God has to give. In Jesus' time, this meekness referred to those whose hearts were open and ready to accept Him as Lord and to receive all the resulting blessings He had to offer. We desire the spiritual inheritance of that accepting spirit—to be humble disciples, open to all the gifts that are ours through Christ.

The third blessing corresponds especially well to the Fourth Step in the Twelve Step recovery programs. Terence T. Gorski in his book *Understanding the Twelve Steps,* writes the following:

> The First Step teaches [those in recovery] . . . that addictive use is destroying their lives. The Second Step teaches them they lack the expert knowledge and the strength to solve the problem or addiction by themselves. The Third Step shows them that there is a source of courage, strength, and hope and a body of technical know-how that can show them the way out.
>
> Now they are ready for Step Four, learning how to take a [personal] inventory. . . . The Fourth Step is designed to humble people. It is designed to show them who they really are in both their strengths and weaknesses. Then they can build upon those strengths while working to overcome the weaknesses.

Because it depends on humility, the Fourth Step is very difficult for many people to take. They consistently linger on Step Three and put off the process of making "a searching and fearless moral inventory" of themselves as Step Four requires. This step is best accomplished in writing, as a serious exercise in discovering just how much the trait of humility needs to be cultivated in us, at this time and in a lasting way.

Notice how all of the blessings, like all of the Twelve Steps, require a trust in God that means we are not doing it all ourselves. We are truly blessed, we are truly in recovery, when God is welcomed into all areas of our life: our thoughts, our desires, our hopes, and our goals. And when we have in mind not only our own well-being but that of our neighbor, then we will see an increased spread of the good news from our lives through a network of sharing Christ's love.

Charles Wesley wrote these poetic lines that could apply to the fellowship of recovery as well as to the church of which we are a part in Christ:

Why hast thou cast our lot
   In the same age and place,
And why together brought
   To see each other's face:
To join in loving sympathy,
And mix our friendly souls in thee?

Didst thou not make us one,
   That we might one remain,
Together travel on,
   And bear each other's pain;

Till all thy utmost goodness prove,
And rise renewed in perfect love?

Why are we with these family members, these neighbors and coworkers, these colleagues, and these recovery fellowship members if not partly to learn this difficult trait of humility? Through humility we share in the life of Christ, who humbled Himself for us and for our salvation:

> He humbled Himself and became obedient to the point of death, even the death of the cross. Therefore God also has highly exalted Him and given Him the name which is above every name, that at the name of Jesus every knee should bow, of those in heaven, and of those on earth, . . . that every tongue should confess that Jesus Christ is Lord, to the glory of God the Father (Phil. 2:8–11).

This is where true, heart-felt humility finds its inspiration and power in Christ. Christ is Lord of all. We are all in this together or not at all. The good news is for me, right now; but it is also for others. When we are bogged down in the midst of life's many petty humiliations and distractions, we can easily lose sight of this truth and this hope. Therefore we are positioned here with one another, for better or worse, to hold up another, and sometimes to allow another to hold us through times of doubt and fear.

If we slow down, we also will become quiet. We will be able to hear the cries of others, not just our own frenzied thrashing about to "do something, quick!" Slow motion will teach us the important trait of caution. It may be one factor that will set us on the path to wisdom as we take time to read and study God's Word and other wise writings that can feed our souls.

When we are in doubt, "easy does it" is always good advice. The simple solution to a problem may be closer than we think; an answer may be at our door even now. Or perhaps nothing needs to be done until our heads are straight about what is true and what is edifying.

Being slow to anger is always a good example of recovery behavior at its best. If we can learn that lesson alone, as a quality of meekness, we will clear our hearts and minds further to receive or "inherit" the goodness of peace and serenity in the days to come.

In the following blessings we will see other traits that mark the people of God and give us a preview of the quality of life God has prepared for us.

Afterthought

God is God, and we're not. From this standpoint, true wisdom can begin. We can let ourselves fail (we will, anyway, from time to time), pick ourselves up, and go on to do the next thing.

We have this virtue—patience—in common with God. From him patience begins; from him its glory and its dignity take their rise. The origin and greatness of patience proceed from God as its author. Man ought to love [this] thing which is dear to God. . . .

—St. Cyprian, *On Patience*

Pray: *Lord, teach me the patience of humility today. Show me both who I am before You; and also, Your love for me. Give me quietness of spirit in the knowledge that You will bring about Your rule over all things in Your time. Amen.*

CHAPTER 4

YOU WILL BE FILLED

Blessed are those who
hunger and thirst
for righteousness,
For they shall
be filled.

What you beg of God,
work also diligently
for it.

JESUS said, "I am the light of the world."

—John 9:5

PUTTING away lying, "Let each one of you speak truth with his neighbor," for we are members of one another.

—Ephesians 4:25

TO thee, O God, we turn for peace . . . but grant us too the blessed assurance that nothing shall deprive us of that peace, neither ourselves, nor our foolish, earthly desires, nor wild longings, nor anxious cravings. . . .

—Søren Kierkegaard
Journals

COMPASSION is the basis of all morality.

—Arthur Schopenhauer

LINDA Neukrug, of Walnut Creek, California, wrote in the October 1991 issue of *Guideposts* magazine of her experience of sharing her resources.

While working at two jobs, she often despaired when she observed homeless people on the San Francisco streets as she walked to and from work. "Sometimes near payday I barely had enough money for bus fare, yet I felt bad as I walked past a sea of outstretched palms."

One day as she made her lunch, she found she had some extra ingredients, so she made a second sandwich. A small act, but one with amazing consequences. That day, when a shabbily clothed man outside her office building asked for spare change, she asked, "Would you like a sandwich?"

His eyes lit up; she had made his day. The next day, she made another sandwich for another homeless person. It was such a simple, easy thing, that Linda continued the habit of "a sandwich a day" to give away, without thinking much about it.

Then one morning a young woman came up to her as she was leaving and tugged on her sleeve. "I wanted you to know that I happened to see what you did, and I decided to do the same thing," the woman told her. And she pulled out an extra foil-wrapped sandwich.

"But it was just one little sandwich," said Linda.

The woman smiled. "But you set one big example," she said.

Have you ever seen your own hunger and thirst to do the right thing become a stream of kindness that turns into a wave of blessings beyond your original thought or effort?

"It is good for us to think no grace or blessing truly ours, till we are aware that God has blessed someone else with it through us," wrote Phillips Brooks. Are we seeing these kinds of results in our life of recovery? Are we a walking illustration of what other people can discover of God, of truth, and of reasonable, lasting peace?

The farther we come in our program of recovery through working the Twelve Steps and seeking serenity in our lives, the more we will find ourselves able to accomplish for the sake of God and others. As we cease to deny that we are imperfect, that we fail, and that we have not done those things we ought to have done, we will begin to find new avenues of genuine service and encouragement to others.

The fourth blessing of which Jesus speaks challenges us to look outward at the world around us—its injustices, its need to hear the truth told, and its opportunities for caring. "Blessed are those who hunger and thirst for righteousness," our Lord said. And Mother Teresa has said, in a wise and realistic reminder to all of us who seek this blessing, "We can do no great things; only small things with great love."

What is it that we are called to work on in order to know the blessing of fulfillment and the strength of God's purpose in our lives?

Jesus calls us first to obedience, to do the work He Himself did while He was on earth. He told His disciples, "He who believes in Me, the works that I do he will do also; and greater works than these he will do. . . . If you ask anything in My name, I will do it" (John 14:12, 14).

What a promise of power and support for our prayers, our desire to serve God, and our work in the world! Jesus fully expected His disciples—and us—to carry on His ministry, bringing healing and peace to a troubled world.

But we need to remember, as people in recovery, that we can only reach for righteousness one day at a time, and usually one act at a time. God is calling us to have a great love—for God, for Christ, and for those around us in need. Such love is a gift, one we can pray to experience every day in the greatest measure that we can receive.

And we must seek to avoid the temptation, as we do good works, to fall into grandiosity—a peril common to recovering people. At some point of exuberant success, we may think *we* can save the world! Thus, even if our original intentions were good, we may undo our own blessing by making too much of ourselves and by failing to rely wholly on God to bring about the result.

As we see in Jesus' blessings, such work begins with our own poverty, our own helplessness—our own hunger and thirst for Jesus' qualities in our lives. It is in humility and dependence on God that we long for others also to seek God and to discover the One who works for good in the lives of those who turn to Him. We share the good news of the gospel to encourage others to trust the Lord, who is always faithful, and to contribute their own labors for the good of all.

Psalm 1 speaks of the righteous person whose "delight is in the law of the LORD":

> And in His law he meditates day
> and night.
> He shall be like a tree
> Planted by the rivers of water,
> That brings forth its fruit in its season,
> Whose leaf also shall not wither;
> And whatever he does shall prosper (vv. 2–3).

God will bless the efforts of those who hunger and thirst after righteousness. The second part of Jesus' word of blessing says that they "shall be filled." This is the abundant life of which He spoke in John 10:10: "I have come that they may have life, and that they may have it more abundantly." He means life here and now, within our own bodies, with our individual limitations—but also with the gifts and talents each of us has that are waiting to be discovered and used.

How closely this parallels our experiences in recovery. We may be learning not only that life is livable once again, not only that we can survive the conditions in which we are placed with our own particular history of deficits and pluses; but also that we can rejoice and give thanks for these blessings.

We have learned to seek God more and more through whatever we face. And we have a growing history of finding peace within our circumstances even as we work to make them better for ourselves and others.

The Anglican writer Jeremy Taylor expressed it well in the following statement: "Whatsoever we beg of God, let us also work for it." Once we see how much the world needs righteousness and justice, we know that we just can't sit back. We must put our hand to the plow, along with others who try to live fruitful lives, using the gifts that we all are given.

Yet, as Scripture reminds us, it is always God who gives the increase, who makes the seed of righteousness grow into a tree of shelter for many, and who nurtures the mustard seed of our faith until it becomes the mightiest of bushes, a miracle from very small beginnings.

How small can our faith be and still be effective?

One person in recovery likened it to being barely able to lift his little finger in response to God's offer to save and renew and restore his life from alcoholism. Yet it was enough. His testimony of a glowing ten years of recovering and bringing others with him proves how little it takes initially, if we hunger and thirst for life and turn to God for help.

Some who hunger and thirst for truth in our time may have great vision and thus be called to do more widespread work to bring about justice and peace.

Edgar Stoesz tells this story:

> The kingdom of heaven can be illustrated by three persons who learned of the prospects of global starvation.
>
> The first said, "We can't feed the world. They shouldn't have so many children. They should work harder and make better use of their land like we do. Nature will maintain its balance and if that means millions will die, I'm sorry. I can't help it."
>
> The second said, "The facts are sobering, and I'm truly sorry, but what can one person do? I can eat less and use less energy, but how could that extra bit of food or energy help millions in India? I wish I could be more helpful."
>
> The third said, "This isn't right. We must change our ways. We must use less, and give

and grow more. We must provide generous support to efforts which increase production and control population. We must urge our governments to reduce military expenditure and increase humanitarian aid. We must reorder our priorities, believing that God wants all his children to live in dignity and self-respect."

Then Jesus asked the three to appear before him. To the first he said, "You selfish fool. You saw people starve and did nothing. Your preoccupation with material things kept you from comprehending the seriousness of the issue. You continued to live in ease while others suffered. You don't deserve to be called my child because you saw need and did nothing."

To the second he said, "Your intentions were good and you even seemed on the verge of understanding the problem, but in the end you rationalized it away. You found release from your guilt, but instead of doing what was within your capacity you added your weight to the forces of helplessness, thereby making it more difficult for others to act."

To the third he said, "I'm pleased. You not only understood, you responded in a practical and helpful way. You did not waste your time

> making up excuses and rationalizations, but responded with the limited resources at your command. You set an example which made it easier for others to respond and, because of what you did, not only were lives saved but many were helped to see my glory" (from the Mennonite Central Committee, Food Production and Rural Development as quoted in *Synthesis*).

To carry this modern parable one step further, surely Jesus also said to the third, resourceful person, "Well done, good and faithful servant; you have been faithful over a few things, I will [give you responsibility] over many things. Enter into the joy of your lord" (Matt. 25:23).

Each of us has been given a little—some more energy than others, some more talents than others, some more zeal than others, some more stamina than others. But as we hunger and thirst after the righteousness that comes from God and returns to God, we will see more people being filled, fewer people being oppressed, and a growing fellowship of twice-born people who are able to reach out to others with a word of hope.

In this hunger for good to prevail, we will manifest an honesty with self, a sincerity in worship, an integrity of spirit, and a sense of wholeness directed toward God's work in the world—our task. How do we know if we hunger and thirst for righteousness in our lives?

We need to ask ourselves: What do we daydream about? What do we work hardest to accomplish? What are our priorities each day? What values do we teach our children, as situations calling for discernment occur in our lives together each day?

We must stop and look at ourselves, listen to our own voices. Jesus' promised blessings call us to see if the shoe fits. Are we like these happy, joyful, "filled" ones of whom our Lord speaks?

"It matters not what you are thought to be," wrote Publilius Syrus, "but what you are." Are we different people in private, with those who know us best and tolerate us, than we are in public? Are we living a lie? What if people really knew our private faces?

These questions test our levels of hunger and thirst for righteousness and the levels of fulfillment we find in the blessedness God has to give abundantly.

As we beg God for the healing of ourselves and our world, let us also work diligently for it, hand in hand, heart to heart, so that the world itself may praise the Creator.

Afterthought

On the left side of a piece of paper, list three simple things you can do for someone else in the next week. Cross off each task as you complete it. On the right side of the paper, make notes about the results.

How do we discern the signs of [God's] Kingdom?

There, where a just order is sought; there, where human life is respected and a full life is fostered; there, where women and men live in solidarity; there, where the structures of society try to favor "the orphan, the widow and the poor"; there, where human beings have the opportunity to become what God intends them to be; there, the Kingdom of God is at work.

On the contrary, there, where the social system is bound to favor a few in detriment of the majority of the members of society; there, where injustice divides and puts people against people; there, where dictatorial regimes curtail freedom and tread underfoot the fundamental rights of people; there, the anti-kingdom is at work.

—Mortimer Arias
Announcing the Reign

Pray: *Lord, may our appetites for justice and peace on earth grow daily, as we seek to live in serenity moment to moment by Your grace. Amen.*

CHAPTER 5

YOU WILL OBTAIN MERCY

Blessed are the merciful,
For they shall obtain mercy.

In order to keep it, you have to give it away.

IF your brother sins against you, rebuke him; and if he repents, forgive him. And if he sins against you seven times in a day, and seven times in a day returns to you, saying, "I repent," you shall forgive him.

—Luke 17:3–4

IF it be the earnest desire and longing of your heart to be merciful as He is merciful . . . if you desire to communicate every good to every creature that you are able; if you love and practise everything that is good, righteous and lovely for its own sake, because it is good, righteous, and lovely; and resist no evil but with goodness; then you have the utmost certainty that God lives, dwells, and governs in you.

—William Law
The Spirit of Prayer

FEAR less, hope more; whine less, breathe more; talk less, say more; hate less, love more; and all good things are yours.

—Anonymous

POP star Cliff Richard, in his book *Which One's Cliff?,* reports a time when he learned what mercy is. He was visiting a Bihari refugee camp in Bangladesh.

"That first morning, I must have washed my hands a dozen times," he remembers. "I didn't want to touch anything, least of all the people." Everyone in the camp, he explains, was covered with running sores or scabs—even the children.

As he bent down to touch one little boy, mainly to provide a photo opportunity for a nearby photographer, mercy struck him in spite of himself. At first he touched warily. Then another person accidentally stepped on the child's fingers.

"He screamed and, as a reflex, I grabbed him, forgetting his dirt and his sores," Richard recalls. "I remember that warm little body clinging to me and the crying instantly stopping. In that moment I knew I had much to learn about practical Christian loving, but that at least I'd started."

Most of us in recovery will recall that we were able to reach out and find the help we needed because we experienced something like mercy: pure grace raining down on our wounded and unmanageable situations. As Shakespeare reminds us:

> The quality of mercy is not strained;
> It droppeth as the gentle rain from heaven
> Upon the place beneath: it is twice blest,
> It blesseth him that gives and him that takes.

In my case, mercy came in the form of an older woman who saw me struggling in a situation similar to what she herself had gone through years earlier. Her kind, caring suggestion that I seek help in Al-Anon was one drop of mercy that enabled me to survive a cataclysm of pain and loss and to find a fellowship of people who also believe in and practice mercy toward others.

Persons have shown compassion in other ways: perhaps taking time from their own concerns to spend time with us, taking us personally to meetings, loaning us recovery books, giving us shoulders to cry on, and reaching out to us in our despair.

Perhaps they shared some of their own stories or gave some gentle advice, seeing that we were finally of a mind to accept it. "The quality of mercy is not strained"; it seems to flow as it is needed, and it acts like a salve to the spirit when it is applied.

And it is "twice blessed." Perhaps we found in those

people new friends, maybe even sponsors, and they also received blessings through helping us.

When Jesus said, "Blessed are the merciful, for they shall obtain mercy" (Matt. 5:7), He was referring to the spiritual effect of the double blessing that mercy has on both the giver and the receiver.

This principle is that of reciprocity—receiving and returning good for good. When we apply the balm of mercy to someone who is hurting, when we have compassion on that person, there is no end to the good that we unleash in the world, which heals countless others along the way.

Matthew 6:14 applies this principle to forgiveness: "For if you forgive men their trespasses, your heavenly Father will also forgive you." And a warning also comes in Matthew 7: "Judge not, that you be not judged" (v. 1). We learn in recovery that none of us is in a position to judge another. Yet we *are* often in a position to show mercy!

Why should so much depend on our extension of mercy to other people, even those who may have wronged us in the past or those who continue to do evil toward us? Because mercy is a quality of God, and those who are called to share a life of blessedness with God, our Lord and King, are to begin to practice here and now some of the rules of His reign.

Jesus showed the unique quality of mercy at work in the parable of the good Samaritan in Luke 10:30–

36. In this story, a man was traveling from Jerusalem to Jericho. On the way, he fell among thieves who took all he had—even his clothes. They wounded him and left him for dead.

Jesus describes the people who came by and their reactions to the plight of the poor victim. A priest, supposedly a holy person, passed right by. Then a Levite, schooled in the Law—but obviously not in mercy—also saw him and went on.

But a certain Samaritan, a person who was "from the wrong side of the tracks" according to the Jews' way of thinking, also came along. This person had compassion on the man.

This man didn't ask whether he was responsible for another, nor did he worry about being paid for his kindness, nor did he fret about the precious time he might be losing on the way to attend to his own concerns. Instead, he tenderly bandaged the man's wounds, took him to an inn, and paid for the victim's recovery.

And who in this story, Jesus asked, was the merciful one?

This simple story we have heard many times contains a profound truth also expressed in Jesus' blessings, one which can and *must* be lived here and now. Jesus calls us to a blessed life of mercifulness toward all those who may appear in our own path.

In this He echoed the ancient wisdom about right living found in Micah 6:8: "He has shown you, O man, what is good; and what does the LORD require of you but to do justly, *to love mercy,* and to walk humbly with your God?" (italics added).

Both the Hebrew tradition and Jesus' own example of giving His life for us while we were still sinners emphasize the importance of mercy.

The extension of mercy to others is the kind of exchange that most pleases God. It is a commerce of the spirit, in which we do not count the actual cost or keep a tally of who owes what to whom. Rather it is a generosity of understanding and action that proceeds naturally from the fact that we ourselves have received mercy from God. Jesus told His followers, "Freely you have received, freely give" (Matt. 10:8).

Truly this is a key to the power behind mercifulness. In our own experiences of being "rescued" mercifully, why were loving people able to extend mercy? Because they had learned (or were learning) that in order to keep it, they had to give it away. In fact, the last of the Twelve Steps reminds us that these people who are practicing the blessing of mercy are those who have had a "spiritual awakening."

They are in the business of carrying this message to other hurting people as they go about their normal lives. By the grace of God, they have been enabled to see things in a wider perspective. They have learned who their neighbors are. And they see that the most important economics in life are the exchanges of mercy, tenderness, compassion, and true concern—person to person, in the name of God.

Why do we need to practice mercy in order to obtain mercy? Because such giving quite naturally will prepare us to grow as we should and enable us to receive even more from God. As we try to follow these guidelines from the gospel, God enlarges our own capacity to give and receive.

Applying such truths may seem foreign to us initially, especially if we have been in a position of protecting ourselves from others' assaults, lies, and attempts to take what is rightfully ours. Yet the Bible affirms that the practice of mercy must begin here, where we are. As we accept this truth on faith and learn to become merciful even in the face of losses and sadness, God promises blessing.

At first, showing mercy is almost like learning a new language, a new way of relating to life, or a fresh set of values. William Temple wrote, "The world, as we live in it, is like a shop window into which some mischievous person has gotten in overnight and shifted all the price labels so that the cheap things have the high price labels on them and the really precious things are priced low."

What qualities seem to have a high value in our society? Success, money, fame, and the aggressive, me-first behavior that enables one person to climb up on the backs of others in order to become first and best.

What attributes seem to be lowly and without reward or recognition in this life? Gentleness, servanthood, compassion, caring for those who cannot care for themselves. *What has happened to our moral and spiritual price tags? Who switched them when we weren't looking?*

In the blessings, Jesus calls us, as He called those in His day, to recognize the true value of other people and to cherish the things that are genuinely worth something. Mercy is a cornerstone of the life in recovery—as it is for any person seeking peace and serenity. How can we ever find peace with God if we cannot see the value of our neighbors all around us who suffer as we do?

Recovery for us means getting the right price tags back on the right qualities of behavior. It involves a reordering of our goals and values toward the way things really are in God's view, which is the world of true values that surrounds us and compels us.

The time for mercy toward ourselves and toward others (for if we are to treat our neighbors as ourselves, then we must first be merciful to ourselves) is *today*. Today is always the day of salvation.

Helmut Thielicke, in *The Waiting Father,* writes, "We should not be concerned primarily to be 'just' to our neighbor, but rather to love and support him. And this we can do only if we are ready to forgive. And I can be ready to forgive only if I have learned that Jesus Christ has forgiven my sins and given me another chance."

So the reciprocity of mercy, forgiveness, and reconciliation one with another is always a gift. It really is a grace that comes from God. It is not a creation of our own goodwill—however strong and loving we may feel at times in our growing life of recovery. If we ever forget our vital connection to the Source of mercy, we will start to sink—as Peter did when he tried to walk on water with diminishing faith in his steps.

We must look continually to God, who enables us to stand, to walk, and to run the course before us. The apostle James calls us to practice "the wisdom that is from above," which is "pure, then peaceable, gentle, willing to yield, *full of mercy* and good fruits, without partiality and without hypocrisy. Now the fruit of righteousness is sown in peace by those who make peace" (3:17–18, italics added).

How beautifully these verses capture the spirit of the blessings! What we have learned of our dependence on God, the need to accept the reality of our circumstances (even when they cause mourning), the essence of humility, the importance of righteousness that bears fruit, and the primacy of mercy—all are reflected here in a picture of what life in harmony with God and others is meant to be.

One of our tasks then, is to put the right price tags back where they belong. How can we?

What qualities shine in our lives that will attract others to the fellowship of recovery and to God's love? How do we express the gentleness of mercy, the power of forgiveness, and the spirit of reconciliation in our life with others?

The urgency of the need for mercy also is evident in Jesus' phrasing of this blessing. If we are to become people who can receive the quality of mercy that God desires to give us, then we must of necessity become merciful creatures.

If we do not begin to "give it away" in our lives whenever we have opportunity, we may find ourselves unable to understand what mercy is. We don't want to lose what we have gained up to this point in recovery. So we will continue to seek creative and consistent opportunities to "give it away"!

Afterthought

When have we experienced unexpected mercy? When have we been compelled to offer mercy to another, quite beyond our original intentions?

True mercy involves several dimensions:

Pardoning one's neighbor (see Matt. 18:21–35).
Aiding the needy (see Matt. 25:31–46).
Helping one's enemies (see Matt. 5:44–47).

When we do, inevitably, fail to live up to the command to show mercy, this prayer adapted from Al-Anon will remind us: "Lord, please forgive me for being judgmental, seeking retaliation, and holding grudges. Help me to forgive myself first; then I will be able to give and forgive others. Amen."

Pray: *Lord, help me, increasingly, to see things as they really are, to affirm Your values, and to show mercy as You have shown mercy to me—filled to the brim, pressed down, and overflowing. Amen.*

CHAPTER 6

YOU WILL SEE GOD

Blessed are the
pure in heart,
For they shall
see God.

Bring the body, and
the mind will follow.

THE heart of the giver makes the gift dear and precious.

—Martin Luther

WHERE does God dwell? . . . God dwells wherever man lets him in.

—Samuel H. Dresner
Prayer, Humility and Compassion

WHO may ascend into the hill of the LORD?
Or who may stand in His holy place?
He who has clean hands and a pure heart.

—Psalm 24:3–4

TO adapt ourselves with a quiet mind to what is possible and attainable, therein lies happiness.

—*One Day at a Time in Al-Anon*

IT may be hard," wrote C. S. Lewis in *Mere Christianity,* "for an egg to turn into a bird; it would be a jolly sight harder for it to learn to fly while remaining an egg!" He goes on: "We are like eggs at present. And you cannot go on indefinitely being just an ordinary decent egg. We must be hatched or go bad."

If we let God bring about this transformation in our lives, God "will make the feeblest and filthiest of us into . . . a dazzling, radiant creature, pulsating all through with such energy and joy and wisdom and love as we cannot imagine. . . .

"The process will be long and, in parts, very painful; but that is what we are in for. Nothing less," Lewis continues.

To turn from an egg into a bird that can soar!

Clearly, the kind of life to which God calls us is one worth seeking. Yet seeking it does not mean trying to be perfect. In our recovery probably we have discovered already that perfectionism is a dead-end road. We know that to find any kind of lasting serenity and happiness, we must first commit ourselves to God and then learn to adapt ourselves to what is possible, what is attainable, and what God has for us.

In fact, it is even possible to undermine our own health and well-being through an unrealistic striving to do everything exactly right each time. In the past, we may have driven ourselves and those around us a bit crazy with our attempts to become perfect and above reproach in relationships, in our jobs, and in our personal images.

What we are called to instead, in peace and openness, is simply to be quiet before God and to seek God's face—for that is where we find true purity of heart. In that place, we will better learn to pray and work for what is needful, what is appropriate, and what is attainable in this minute, this hour, or this day.

In Jesus' sixth blessing He points us to this truth. He even says that the pure in heart will see God. The word *heart* here can refer to the mind or the intellect, in the Hebrew way of thinking. It has everything to do with our attitudes and our choices, as these too will affect how we are able to pray. What we allow into our consciousness becomes part of us, the essence of our personhood and values.

In Psalm 77:6 we find a shade of meaning: "I call to remembrance . . . I meditate within my heart, and my spirit makes diligent search." This deep, heart thinking is that to which Jesus referred.

What we truly are as we are quiet and receptive in our innermost heart before God is the basis for our attitudes, our choices, and our behavior. And it is a preparation for the persons we are becoming as well. We are told in this blessing to prepare ourselves for the way things can be—that the pure in heart will fellowship with God, now and in the future.

This desire for purity calls us (as well as we can live it) to a life of justice, fidelity, loyalty to God's commands, and sincerity of worship—values understood by Jesus' audience to be part of the Law and of God's way. Yet in Jesus' teaching, keeping the Law is never enough.

In recovery probably we have discovered already a similar truth. Rules and principles, as important as they are, are never enough. We can't accomplish recovery perfectly, or even at all, on our own. Yet if we will bring our hearts, minds, and bodies to God for healing and help, God will accomplish it through us.

This is humility before God, a true serenity of spirit and a kind of innocence or purity of intention that will get us much farther than pride in doing everything right. A humble attitude requires knowing ourselves (as much as possible) as God knows us, accepting our limitations and our assets, and getting on with what we *can* do to live in God's ways.

In James 4:8 we discover how important it is to be of one mind within ourselves in order to experience this peace or fellowship with God. "Draw near to God and He will draw near to you. Cleanse your hands . . . and *purify your hearts,* you double-minded" (italics added). It is clear that being of two minds—having begun recovery but wavering, seeking God but trying to hold onto ourselves, saying one thing but thinking another—all these duplicities of mind war against the kind of purity and wholeness of which Jesus—and the psalmist and James—speaks.

What does it take to discover and practice true single-mindedness? We must exercise a disciplined focus on the truth of our situations. As we have seen earlier, sometimes our response will entail grief, mourning—and always humility.

James continues, "Lament and mourn and weep! Let your laughter be turned to mourning and your joy to gloom" as you face reality and what it may require of you in order to grow in purity. Then, "Humble yourselves in the sight of the Lord, and He will lift you up" (4:10). Notice how these admonitions echo the earlier blessings. James shows that bringing about the blessedness of which Jesus speaks is always the work of God and not of ourselves.

Perhaps in our lives recently—in the midst of family fights, unemployment, illnesses, economic woes, or foiled plans—all we have been able to do is drag ourselves up in the morning to face another day. Yet in God's mercy, that is enough.

"Bring the body, and the mind will follow," we are told in A.A. and Al-Anon. Are we bringing ourselves face to face with other people whom we might help, even as we seek to help ourselves? Are we taking our tired and sometimes indifferent selves to meetings so that we are in a position to receive inspiration and support? Are we attending church—even if it means sitting and waiting for a miracle of grace which as yet seems unimaginable to our rational minds?

All of these are realistic avenues to the kind of purity of heart and the single-mindedness of belief that is part of healthy thinking and living.

What do we think about as we wait to receive the check in the mail, or anticipate the phone call, or look for time to get everything done? We will find God where our hearts are, if we have asked the Lord to be present with us—even in experiences of loss, failure, struggle, or pain. Like the friends traveling the road to Emmaus in the gospel of Luke who found Jesus, the risen Lord, in their company, we will find that He is with us as well.

Read the Gospels and discover the many ways Jesus brought healing and insight to His followers and countless others to whom He spoke when He was on earth. Where He was, things happened; people were changed; the work of God grew.

Bring your body to the place where it should be, and the experience will enhance your mind and your capabilities. God will work because you have made this effort to be in the right place for the right reason.

John Sanford writes in *The Kingdom Within:*

> The kingdom of heaven begins in a person's life as something seemingly small and insignificant but through a process of growth becomes a mighty power. The image of the tree is appropriate, for just as a tree is rooted in the earth but reaches up to heaven, so [our growth] includes both our earthly and our spiritual natures. . . . Because the kingdom is associated with the inner growth of the individual, it is very much a here-and-now experience.

What if the seed for the tree were not placed properly? In Jesus' parable of the sower and the different types of ground (see Mark 4:3–20), we see how important the right environment is for growth and nurture.

Thus our own spiritual lives grow through our placement in the world for service and transformation of life.

We can learn much from our own children in this regard. They don't sit down and figure out exactly how everything is going to work out before they begin to pick up toys or objects and use them, before they play or listen or observe. They follow their hearts—throw themselves into activities with all their energies and discover along the way (in *serendipity*) what they can learn from their experience. Too often as adults we think we have to know all the ins and outs of every action and its consequences. Yet we can never know all of those things ahead of time.

However, we can take the first step of obedience by placing ourselves in a position to be taught and to change. Keep an open mind. Listen and learn. For some it may mean breaking away from a destructive relationship—physically removing oneself from being another person's victim.

It may mean taking jobs for less pay so that we can become whole in mind and body by using our talents according to God's values and not the world's. It may mean admitting that we were wrong and losing face. Such an admission, when it is true, will eventually put us in a new position of strength.

All correct "placement" is going to bring about further wholeness and what Jesus calls purity because it more nearly represents the truth about ourselves and our lives. Thus we will find ourselves in a position to grow, to become conscious of what we have been doing to ourselves or to others, and to stop. We will be enlarged and enriched, open to further understanding of the work we are uniquely called to do.

John Ruskin wrote, "If you want to work for this Kingdom of God, and to bring it, and enter into it, there is just one condition to be first accepted. You must enter it as a child or not at all."

Purity of heart has a close relationship to the innocence or guilelessness of children. Jesus also said to be "wise as serpents and harmless as doves" (Matt.

10:16). We are not children; we have had experiences that have led us to this point. We have known failure and perhaps even despair which has impelled us to seek recovery and to seek God's face. Therefore our purity or harmlessness is not ignorance or naïveté. It is a true simplicity of spirit that comes through seeking only God and God's purposes for us, "praying only for knowledge of His will for us and the power to carry that out" (Step Eleven).

One reason this purity of heart is so hard to describe is that people must enter into it wholly before they can taste and find it is good. It is not a reward or a sign of having achieved above our peers to find such closeness to God, to be able to "see God"—to know and desire the divine will more fully. If we think we are more advanced than others, we have missed the point entirely and have hardly begun to understand purity.

Purity of heart is simply life as we are meant to live it: more abundantly, less self-defeating, more joyously, richer and in deeper fellowship with others who also seek God's face. This is blessing, and this is life in the purity of spirit to which Jesus both calls us and leads us.

AFTERTHOUGHT

Draw a "map" of where you are in your life of recovery. Make it in the shape of a maze, if you wish. Where do you want to go? What do you call that place? Draw it and put in the steps along the path that take you there with God's help. Use the Twelve Steps as a guideline if you wish; or use some of the recovery principles in your own words to describe resting places of the soul that you seek.

Pray: *Be thou a light unto my eyes, music to mine ears, sweetness to my taste, and full contentment to my heart. Be thou my sunshine in the day, my food at table, my repose in the night, my clothing in nakedness, and my succour in all necessities. Lord Jesu, I give thee my body, my soul, my substance, my fame, my friends, my liberty and my life. Dispose of me and all that is mine as it may seem best to thee and to the glory of thy blessed name.*

—John Cosin (1594–1672)
Bishop of Durham

CHAPTER 7

YOU WILL BE A CHILD OF GOD

Blessed are the peacemakers,
For they shall be called sons of God.

Learn to arbitrate; agree to disagree. If two people agree about everything, at least one is unnecessary.

LORD, make me an instrument of your peace;
where there is hatred let me sow love,
where there is injury let me sow pardon,
where there is doubt let me sow faith,
where there is despair let me give hope,
where there is darkness let me give light,
where there is sadness let me give joy.

—attributed to St. Francis

A soft answer turns away wrath,
But a harsh word stirs up anger.
The tongue of the wise uses knowledge rightly.

—Proverbs 15:1–2

NO longer be children, tossed to and fro and carried about with every wind . . . but, speaking the truth in love [we] may grow up in all things into Him who is the head—Christ—from whom the whole body, joined and knit together . . . [so that] every part does its share, causes growth of the body . . . in love.

—Ephesians 4:14–16

ROBERT D. Lupton writes in his book *Theirs Is the Kingdom* of a saint who lives in his neighborhood. "I call her the Mother Teresa of Grant Park," he says.

> She has been an inner-city missionary for nearly thirty years. She has no program, no facility, and no staff. She lives in virtual poverty. Her house blends well with the poor who are her neighbors. There are box springs and mattresses on the porch and grass growing up around the old cars in her front yard.
>
> She goes about feeding and clothing the poor with donations from concerned people. She works all hours of the day and night. She is difficult to reach by phone, and she doesn't give tax-deductible receipts to her donors.

Yet she is, by her life and example, by her position of service within her own inner-city world, a true peacemaker. She stands between those who have something to give, and those who need it. She makes the connection between the two, yet she never counts the cost.

Perhaps we are not called to such a radical role of meeting people's needs and furthering life in such dramatic ways. Yet it is consistent with our goal of recovery and service to discover how we as children of God are called to be peacemakers in the world around us.

Peacemakers are also individuals who arbitrate on behalf of the truth, who seek to bring two parties into cordial agreement and enable life to go on. This may be done—and must be attempted—at all levels of society; within families, among workers, and in the nations of the world.

To be a peacemaker is a noble calling and one at which some people have great skill: an easy manner of conciliatory speech and actions that bring consistent results. Other people, however, seem to create dissension wherever they go: they polarize groups, stir up discontent, and bring disharmony into any situation.

The division of people into these two groups looks, on the surface, to be so simple. Some are peacemakers and therefore right. Others are wrong. But our experiences in recovery call us to look more closely at this concept of peacemaking.

When Jesus said in this seventh blessing, "Blessed are the peacemakers," was He really referring to a kind of peacemaking that will always make everyone happy? It seems doubtful that the Mother Teresa of

Grant Park would be popular to everyone any more than was that desert dissenter, John the Baptist.

As with Jesus himself, those called to bring a more lasting peace will seldom please everyone. Any reading of the Gospels will show us that disruption can be a sign of God's working, too. Jesus even said that He came not to bring peace, but a sword (see Matt. 10:34). He knew that the gospel would not only heal but also divide people.

The kind of "peace" that ignores difficult realities is not only impossible but also undesirable. When you look at the real dynamics of any group—a family, a company, a church—you find that true peacemaking takes more than keeping members perpetually happy.

As Christians and as people in recovery, we are challenged to be truth-tellers—open to uncovering what the real situation is in any conflict and willing to describe what we see. But we are also wholly dedicated to whatever course of action will benefit the whole body.

The biblical metaphor of a body with various parts that perform different necessary functions expresses beautifully how interconnected and interdependent we are in Christ. This is our starting point for understanding and living in reconciliation, for practicing true peacemaking.

What any one of us does affects all the others; and since we are children of God, we are also accountable to God and to one another for any actions that hurt the body. Moreover, in Ephesians Paul tells us also to grow up (see 4:15); to be "no longer children"—in the sense of being people who are easily swayed—who thereby fall prey to the aggressive and overpowering forces of evil in the world. Though we must be like children in other positive ways, we are called to take an adult stand in the world.

And we are to speak the truth in love. This action, as many of us have learned and are continuing to learn, will cost us something. People who dare to speak the truth are not always popular. Just look at the track record of the Old Testament prophets. Whenever they proclaimed the word of the Lord to the straying people of their day, they found persecution and were often silenced by wicked rulers and rivals.

Yet we are continuing to learn that getting at the truth demands dialogue, dedication, and a desire for peace and serenity for everyone concerned. Many people in dysfunctional families may have developed very pleasant and agreeable personalities through their growing-up years in order to survive, in order to avoid conflict and be "liked." Yet through the years, their reluctance to express themselves in true, opinioned voices in their families may have subtly increased their anger within. This kind of silent suffering in the hopes of not making others mad at us is not what Scripture means by true peacemaking.

People who now describe themselves as codependent may just be realizing that they also had ideas and needs and points of view that they were unable or afraid to express in the past for fear of losing what little security they might have felt. Especially if they lived with an alcoholic or excessively angry or oppressive parent, they may never have discovered any opening to express their own needs, thoughts, and ideas.

They learned to bite their tongues when they saw abuse, whether it was abuse of others or of themselves. Thus they unconsciously cooperated with a sick system, out-of-sync families, and perhaps later found themselves in unbalanced marriages or unfair working environments in which they had no idea how to negotiate their position.

When our consciousness grows in the context of recovery—as well as in our spiritual and devotional lives—we discover that it is no longer acceptable for us to keep silent in the face of serious problems, disagreements, and abusive behavior. We find that we are called on to learn (for some of us, very late in life) how to negotiate. We must learn to arbitrate; agree to disagree. This concept scares some people who have feared dissension and the overreactions of addicted people with whom they have lived. Some addicted people can nearly explode whenever they experience opposition, problems, or failures. And the codependents who are vitally connected to them usually get the worst of the fallout.

One young woman recalls her feelings:

> I used to try to keep bad things from happening to my husband, because his anger was so severe that we all felt wounded when he went crazy over a stalled car or a lost checkbook. I resorted to ridiculous efforts to try to make the home environment "perfect" so he wouldn't have anything to get angry at us about. But, of course, being human, I failed constantly. And I blamed myself. It never occurred to me that he was the one who needed to change within himself. I thought I had to make my marriage work at any cost.

True peace between two people can only come when they desire it and are willing to work toward it; or when one or both are willing to grow to the place where they can share serenity. This doesn't mean agreement on every issue. How colorless life would be if we never had differing opinions or even legitimate arguments over how to do something. What many never learned growing up is that disagreements do not have to be expressed in threatening or abusive ways. Difference is the spice of life if it can be expressed in love and reasonableness for the growth of the whole body, not just for the satisfaction or ego of the one who "wins."

If two people agree about everything, at least one is unnecessary. Each member of the body has a function, a role to play, an opinion to give which can affect and enrich the whole family system, church congregation, work crew, or office staff. In an environment of true peace, each person should feel free to express those opinions and to admit needs, doubts, worries (as long as those admissions do not constitute subtle ammunition against another person). Each member should be able to find support for his or her sincere, personal search for truth.

We were each created for a unique purpose. But we are all called to be instruments of God's peace in the world in whatever ways we are suited and empowered. For most peacemakers, kind words and a gentle approach will enable us to negotiate between two opinions and help all involved to find a lasting solution.

"A soft answer turns away wrath," says Proverbs 15:1. It is good advice for most situations. But the Bible also supports our standing up for ourselves in truth: "If your brother sins against you, rebuke him" (Luke 17:3). We have a right to call things what they are and to object to violence and abuse against ourselves and others. Jesus goes on to say, "If he repents, forgive him." This too is part of true reconciliation.

Children generally learn to negotiate as soon as they have a brother or sister. It's either speak up for their rights or get trampled on or left out when the candy's passed around. Adult life doesn't differ much in our need to speak up and let others know that we are part of the situation—that we are human and that we are valuable. How each person learns to do this is the story of a developing personality (and character).

If we have never learned to speak up, to negotiate, to arbitrate, and to reconcile on the basis of the truth, then we must begin to learn in our recovery. Our lesson is a different one from that of the person who tends to be controlling, who says by manner or words, as though all authority rested in him or her: "This is how it's going to be."

Yet these people are extremely valuable to the body as well—if they can learn the lesson from the opposite standpoint. Persons who try to control themselves like dictators and also try to bring other people under that sphere of control, are often those who have succeeded at something and do have skills and gifts to offer the body. But those persons have the task of learning the quietness of speech that comes so easily to the passive person: to step back from wrath and to control anger; to listen instead of talking; to wait before either acting or reacting until the whole story is told.

What is true peace and real peacemaking? It comes close to this idea of negotiating and arbitrating but has satisfying results for all who must live with the decisions that are made. True peace recognizes that we are all meant to enjoy life as children of God.

For the codependents who sought peace at any cost, it was not worth it. It was never real or lasting peace because they had to placate the difficult persons again the next day and try to make reality come out right once again so they could either be left alone or survive the storm. No reciprocity or concern existed for the codependents; their needs didn't exist. Thus they were unable to realize true intimacy.

Controlling persons had no peace either, because the expressed anger itself was a barrier to shut out intimacy and understanding. So both sides were lonely. Codependents needed to become tougher, to learn to construct and protect more definite boundaries of personality; controllers needed to relax rigid borders and to consider others' feelings and needs for the sake of love and true relationship.

For many, this miracle never happened in such a mismatched relationship. For some couples in recovery, true transformation and rebuilding of a life together was possible. Yet perhaps even those whose relationships failed were enabled somehow, with help and through continued stumbling, to recognize such no-win situations in the future. Then they could choose to turn from the impossible demands for "peace" at any cost that certain people might try to place on them.

Perhaps they also realized that their attracting such

people reflected a desire to rework and rewrite the script of a no-win relationship they had in childhood. They even might have acknowledged that in that relationship they were unable to speak up or negotiate—and so eventually became unnecessary. It is a harsh truth to discover.

Yet somehow, underlying this harsh reality, we may discover the blessing of learning what true peacemaking is. It is never too late to decide not to settle for the *semblance* of peace but to seek real relationship in love and reciprocity and equality before God. It is as children of God that we find our true identities in peace and serenity so that we can continue to pray and to mourn for those who as yet have not chosen that peace.

AFTERTHOUGHT

When have I been impelled to take an action that I knew was right but which did not bring immediate peace? When, in another case, could I have expressed peace more effectively by a gentle approach? What have I learned from these experiences?

> Thou our Father, Christ our Brother,
> All who live in love are thine;
> Teach us how to love each other,
> Lift us to the joy divine.
>
> —Samuel Wesley

This famous hymn reminds us of the call to work for peace more broadly; for in the Hebrew thinking about peacemaking the dimension of international harmony goes hand in hand with concerns for inner peace and individual right relationships with God and others. The true peacemaker will actively foster that which leads to peace at all levels.

Pray: *Lord, may I learn what it means for me to be a peacemaker in my life and my individual path of recovery. Help me not to judge people and their level of understanding of peace but to give thanks for the fellowship of all others—with their unique opinions and outlooks. Help me to value what the expression of differing views and experiences can contribute to the nurture of the whole body of which I am part. Amen.*

CHAPTER 8

YOU WILL BE BLESSED AND FORGIVEN

Blessed are those who
are persecuted
for righteousness' sake,
For theirs is the kingdom of
heaven.

Do not judge or retaliate; always forgive yourself first and the forgiveness of others will follow.

IF you love those who love you, what reward have you? Do not even the tax collectors do the same?

I say to you, love your enemies, bless those who curse you, do good to those who hate you, and pray for those who spitefully use you and persecute you.

—Matthew 5:46, 44

WE are asked to forgive those who have injured us. Unless we have first judged and condemned them for what they did, there would be no reason for us to forgive them. Rather we would [first] have to forgive ourselves for judging. . . . [Thus] we can forgive only ourselves. In doing so, we forgive the person whose action we have resented.

—*One Day at a Time in Al-Anon*

YOU are deceived if you think that a Christian can live without persecution. A storm puts a man on his guard and obliges him to exert his utmost efforts to avoid shipwreck.

—St. Jerome

A. PHILIP Parham writes in *Letting God: Christian Meditations for Recovering Persons* of a pastor whose friend lost his little boy to cholera. The boy's father said, "Well, Padre, it is the will of God. That's all there is to it."

To that the minister answered, "Suppose someone came up to your boy and stuck a syringe full of cholera germs into his arm, what would you think of that?"

The father answered that, of course, he would nab the man for murder.

"But my dear friend," the pastor said, "isn't that what you accused God of doing? Didn't you just call God a murderer when you said it was his will? Call your little boy's death the result of mass folly, bad drains and sanitation, carelessness and ignorance—but don't call it the will of God!"

In recovery we have learned that we are to seek to discern what truly is God's will. We are to desire genuine peace in all things. We are not to choose to be victims; such needless suffering is one peril from which our recovery has begun to set us free. Yet even our best efforts will of necessity fail from time to time.

We must constantly take care that we do not punish ourselves for such failures; nor should we be continually blaming others—least of all God—in order to get ourselves off the hook. A more subtle danger, at any point of success in our lives and programs, would be to lose sight of the difficult realities of life in which some strain and even suffering are inevitable.

We don't like to think of having to face future pain as we take a stand in the world for truth and righteousness and peace, as we mourn in solidarity with the poor and needy, as we forgive those who may continue to harm and do evil toward us, and as we forsake personal gains for the sake of the body of Christ.

It would be appealing to think that once we are on the path of recovery and Christian service, we have it made—that others will naturally see what we have to offer, be attracted to it, and choose to walk with us. But we know that this is far from the case. Instead, the Bible is clear that true followers will find persecution and roadblocks in their attempts to live a new life and to seek God's way. As we begin taking steps toward recovery—and our continual surrender to God empowers us to go on—we can be sure that we will find opposition as well.

We will find temptations to get off the track: to become discouraged or to stop attending meetings. Many attitude and behavior problems we have had in the past will appear in new forms. We always need to keep our eyes and ears open to what God is showing and telling us *now:* how to persevere through *these* difficulties.

In Matthew 4, we read that when Jesus had fully committed Himself to do the work of His Father, He also found Himself tempted in the wilderness (a symbol of barrenness and loss). He was tempted to forsake His mission and make selfish choices for His own good rather than to trust God the Father to preserve and direct His life. Yet He persevered through these trials and was not waylaid from the path to the cross.

We too may find ourselves persecuted by others' intentions for us: being told untruths or being thwarted in our desire to do only God's will for us and to find the power to carry it out (Step Eleven). Yet Jesus' eighth word of blessing tells us that we will find blessing even in such hardship and temptation.

"Blessed are those who are persecuted for righteousness' sake." Theologian Oscar Stephen Brooks, in his book *The Sermon on the Mount: Authentic Human Values,* points out that this blessing

> is similar to the fourth one which described the hungering and thirsting ones. In both, the end or object of concern is righteousness or right relation to God. In the previous case the ideal group longs for it; in this case they are willing to be persecuted for it. This stresses the intense commitment of those embodying this

characteristic; they are willing to suffer personally on behalf of their relation to God.

No wonder this most profound and demanding promise of blessing comes at the end of this set of values and admonitions promising joy because of God's action in the life of the believer.

We are called to acknowledge a paradox, to have the kind of eyes to see and ears to hear that the trials and temptations of believers are signs of God's ultimate favor on their lives. It is not an easy concept to swallow or to experience in earnest.

We know from this same chapter in Matthew that we are to pray for those who persecute and unjustly use us (see Matt. 5:44). Yet, as recovering persons, we are not to ask for persecution in order to put into practice these responses, nor are we to seek to acquire enemies to love.

Once I was told by a pastor to forgive someone while that person was still harming me and planning further steps against me. I knew that my gut reactions and instincts for survival were, in that moment, as much a part of my spirituality as was my understanding of what God might require of me. I chose to run as far and as fast as I could from that situation, and I tried to spare my children from its effects as well, taking steps to get away from the oppression.

Therefore, I do not overspiritualize this need to forgive enemies. I believe that sometimes we *must* seek survival rather than continued suffering. Then, eventually, when we become healed of the sharpness of the trauma and the pain of suffering, ways of practicing genuine forgiveness will open up—if we truly seek them. After we are through the crisis and have found some balance in our personal lives again, we will be able to see more clearly exactly what is required of us.

Slowing down, easing off on ourselves, even disregarding unrealistic spiritual demands that well-meaning counselors (or we ourselves) may impose on us is sometimes not a bad thing. Waiting, praying, and seeking further understanding—such a response denies neither the truth of this blessing nor the reality of evil in the world.

It is true that Jesus was able to pray, "Father, forgive them" even as evil people crucified Him. And perhaps we will be given the grace to see beyond our present pain and to experience forgiveness in our hearts right in the midst of oppression.

But we are human—struggling, incomplete—and cannot fully enter into the joy of this blessing in our present lives, in every case, every time. We must not seek perfection in this or any other attribute of the moral or spiritual life here presented in Jesus' visionary Sermon on the Mount and in these eight specific calls to the blessed life.

What our walk in Christ and our recovery will eventually bring about in us is an inner transformation, a profound change in our way of looking at life at the deepest level. We will simultaneously value our lives in Christ more dearly, and we will count our lives as nothing in light of the gospel and following Christ's way.

We will learn to love ourselves in a way that brings light and salt to the world (see Matt. 5:13–14); and miraculously, our self-presence and self-preservation among others will enlighten and preserve many of them and affirm their worth as well.

Poet George Herbert wrote: "Teach me, my God and King, / in all things Thee to see, / and what I do in any thing, / to do it as for thee." This kind of thinking about blessedness, about right relation to God, will gradually begin to permeate our lives so that we are not as conscious of our own service or selflessness or way of life—rather those things will speak for themselves. Our lives will be characterized by the blessedness that Christ promises.

In a sense, the blessings show us that we already have citizenship in heaven, that place which is being prepared even now through our own choices and actions, as well as God's working in and through us.

Matthew 5:11 completes the difficult truth of this last blessing in a way that only makes sense when we keep God's future plans for us in mind: "Blessed are you when they revile you and persecute you, and say all kinds of evil against you falsely for My sake."

Christ Himself suffered the pain of false witness during His lifetime, yet evil people were unable to prevent the accomplishment of His work and the fulfillment of His mission. And ultimately, though we may be waylaid many times, Scripture tells us that "neither death nor life, nor angels nor principalities nor powers, nor things present nor things to come, nor height nor depth, nor any other created thing, shall be able to separate us from the love of God which is in Christ Jesus our Lord" (Rom. 8:38–39).

If we learn to keep a clean slate—an open heart before God each day, confessing our shortcomings and asking for strength to grow into the challenges that present themselves to us—we will be able to endure. If we find ourselves unduly preoccupied with what others are doing to us—how they are preventing us from recovering, making our lives impossible, standing in our way—we may have work to do in forgiving ourselves and learning not to judge others so harshly.

This forgiving state of mind and heart must be practiced diligently before we can find a clearer perspective on whether we are truly being persecuted for righteousness' sake or simply creating our own messes and living in them while blaming other people.

Our sponsor or spiritual mentors can help us see more clearly what we can do in our situation: that we are not powerless; that suffering may be real, but it will not last forever; that we can protect ourselves and those we love from abuse and attack and must do so in order to put a stop to obvious evil.

We need not look for trials or hardships. They will come, in any life. But our relationship to Christ and our heart-receptivity to His blessings can transform how we deal with them. We have everything we need to know of the good and joyful life and its consequences now and in the future—when Jesus Christ is known to be Savior, Ruler, Lord, and King.

AFTERTHOUGHT

God wills that we have life. God intends for us to be healthy. God works and moves his energy toward salvation. Whatever pain, suffering, and disaster befall us are not God's desire.

—A. Philip Parham

I am giving Thee worship with my whole life,
I am giving Thee assent with my whole power,
I am giving Thee praise with my whole tongue,
I am giving Thee honour with my whole utterance.

I am giving Thee love with my whole devotion,
I am giving Thee kneeling with my whole desire,
I am giving Thee love with my whole heart,
I am giving Thee affection with my whole sense,
I am giving Thee my existence with my whole mind,
I am giving Thee my soul, O God of all gods.

—Celtic prayer

EPILOGUE

YOU WILL BE GLAD

Rejoice and be exceedingly glad.

Head and heart together.

GOD'S Power displayed in the world, is nothing but his goodness strongly reaching all things from height to depth . . . and irresistibly imparting itself to every thing.

—Ralph Cudworth, 1647

GOD is the fellow sufferer who understands . . .

—Norman Pittenger, quoting
Alfred North Whitehead

FREEDOM from addiction, like freedom from other forms of bondage which separate us from one another and from God, is just the beginning. Those in recovery learn what St. Augustine learned: that only a relationship with God can fill "the hole in our soul" we've been trying to fill with other things.

—Richard Reid-King

YOUR sorrow will be turned into joy. . . . I will see you again and your heart will rejoice, and your joy no one will take from you. . . . Ask, and you will receive, that your joy may be full.

—John 16:20, 22, 24

BABE Ruth struck out 1,330 times." Thus begins a reflection from the book *In God's Care*. "Fortunately for baseball fans, Babe Ruth didn't let his many strikeouts defeat him. He continued going to bat, and he kept hitting home runs." The rest is history.

The article continues, "We can be pretty certain Babe Ruth didn't define himself as either a total failure *or* a perfect baseball player. He was an ordinary human being with a special talent that he worked to develop. We are no different."

No matter how we may have stumbled or failed in the past; despite any sorrows we have known; and in spite of our situation at the moment, however difficult, these words are for us: "Rejoice and be exceeding glad!"

There is always a reason to look up. Yet the kind of joy to which we are called in our recovery is not a carefree mindlessness of spirit, a lack of concern, come what may. It is a joy that takes into account what is really important in life; a joy that admits the reality of pain and suffering in this world and goes beyond this realization to a peace and serenity in our own particular, given calling.

Somehow, we are to keep an eye on the heavens, while also watching our own footsteps carefully. Living this way will inspire in us the spirit of thankfulness, of joy in all creation in the midst of our recovery—because God is at work in our lives and in the world.

How do Jesus' blessings relate to our goal of growing in peace and harmony with others? Oscar Stephen Brooks in *The Sermon on the Mount* points out that Jesus describes a believer in God as one who "has a distinctive disposition." Here is how the "profile of the ideal person begins to emerge," according to Brooks: "He is one who has had a deep experience [that] has led him to an inner desire to have the right relation to God, and his fellowman." This is both our beginning (Step One) and our end (Step Twelve).

To paraphrase the words of Step Twelve: "Having had a spiritual awakening as the result of these steps, he will try to carry this message to [other people], and to practice these principles in all of his affairs." The person who has the eyes to see and the ears to hear Jesus' message, and who has realized God's love, cannot help but be changed, from deep within, through this experience.

Therefore it is no surprise that the attribute of blessedness with which Jesus Himself ends this section of His sermon is joy. Though we do not have it made and have not found complete healing or total recovery (nor will we, in this life), we grow to understand that "all shall be well, and all shall be well, and all manner of thing shall be well," in the words of the medieval writer Lady Julian of Norwich.

This truth is somewhat poetic, as it involves more than rational understanding. To experience God's "happy ending" we must bring head and heart together. If we think we can logically figure out God and God's purposes in the world, we are headed for defeat. But we can, as the Bible has taught us, worship Almighty God unreservedly, and focus our minds and hearts on the attributes of peace and blessedness that reside in God. This is exactly what we are called to do in our Christian lives, regularly and sincerely.

It is not before, but in the midst of, life that we begin to understand Christian belief, recovery, blessedness, and joy. By entering into what we can affirm of God's goodness in the world and what we have already experienced of it, we turn our past sorrow into unrestrained, overflowing joy.

It is a miracle that works, as so many people will attest—those who have even sadder and more impossible stories of addiction or codependency or personal loss than our own.

The truth of Jesus' invitation here to rejoice—not because everything is dandy, but because God is God, and we may be in relationship with this God—is a sound one. Yet it is often a difficult one. Christians are called on to rejoice even though we have an awareness of evil in the world, of sinfulness and failure in ourselves and others, and of our inability to better ourselves through our own strength.

Perhaps it is through our rejoicing even in the midst of real troubles and heartaches that we are most effective in reaching out to other hurting persons. We know that "there but for the grace of God" go we. We know that in order to grow, we must look within ourselves and begin to work on the principles of recovery that have been made available to us.

We also know that there is always a danger of pride whenever we think we "know" something. Therefore, we must continue to see ourselves as learners, along with others, in order not to lose what we think we already have. This humility is a heart knowledge essential to true joy.

Another secret of joy in recovery is to avoid judging others in a way that lets us off the hook and keeps us from further conviction of our own sins. Johann Tauler, the German spiritual writer, said, "He who desires to become a spiritual man must not be ever taking note of others, and above all of their sins, lest he fall into wrath and bitterness, and a judging spirit towards his neighbours."

Rejoicing in what God has given us, the particular taste of goodness that has been granted to us each day, is a wonderful antidote to such bitterness and a judging spirit. This means consistent, serious attention to the many promises in God's Word that give us reason to rejoice daily, in all things.

And the blessings also compel us to look ahead with the eye of faith to what might be, what should be, and what someday shall be. If we are to experience the peace and serenity to which God calls each person, we will begin to discover it here and now, in the circumstances in which we find ourselves, or not at all.

In his classic work *The City of God,* St. Augustine wrote of a vision of lasting joy that speaks to us poetically of what shall be someday—when God's kingdom fully comes:

> The peace of the celestial city is the perfectly ordered and harmonious enjoyment of God and of one another in God.

In the hope of this promised blessing, we rejoice!

SOURCES

A New Day: Meditations for Personal and Spiritual Growth (New York: Bantam, 1988).

Announcing the Reign of God, by Mortimer Arias (Philadelphia: Fortress Press, 1984).

Believing in Myself: Daily Meditations for Healing and Building Self-Esteem (New York: Prentice Hall, 1991).

His Thoughts Said . . . His Father Said . . . , by Amy Carmichael (Fort Washington, Penn.: Christian Literature Crusade, 1941).

In God's Care: Daily Meditations on Spirituality in Recovery (New York: Hazelden, 1990).

The Kingdom Within, by John A. Sanford (San Francisco: Harper & Row, 1970).

Letting God: Christian Meditations for Recovering Persons, by A. Philip Parham (San Francisco: Harper & Row, 1987).

Mere Christianity, by C. S. Lewis (New York: Macmillan, 1958).

The New Christian Year, by Charles Williams (London: Oxford University Press, 1941).

One Day at a Time in Al-Anon (New York: Al-Anon Family Group Headquarters, Inc., 1968).

The Sermon on the Mount: Authentic Human Values, by Oscar Stephen Brooks (New York: University Press of America, 1985).

Still Life: A Book of Days (Batavia, Ill.: Lion Books, 1989).

Theirs Is the Kingdom, by Robert D. Lupton (New York: Harper & Row, 1989).

The Waiting Father, by Helmut Thielicke (New York: Harper & Row, 1959).

Twelve Months of Days, by David Rioux (Minneapolis: CompCare Publishers, 1990).

Understanding the Twelve Steps, by Terence T. Gorski (New York: Prentice Hall, 1989).

Which One's Cliff? by Cliff Richard (London: Hodder & Stoughton).